Diana
The People's Princess

Richard Wood

WAYLAND

Cover photograph: Diana sitting with a young girl who was the victim of a landmine explosion, in Angola in 1997.
Title page: Diana with her sons, William and Harry, at a children's theme park in 1993.

Editor: Carron Brown
Designer: Malcolm Walker
Production controller: Carol Titchener

First published in 1998 by Wayland Publishers Limited, 61 Western Road, Hove, East Sussex BN3 1JD

© Copyright 1998 Wayland Publishers Limited

Find Wayland on the Internet at http://www.wayland.co.uk

British Library Cataloguing in Publication Data
Wood, Richard
Diana: The People's Princess. – (Famous Lives)
1. Diana, Princess of Wales – Juvenile literature
2. Princesses – Great Britain – Biography – Juvenile literature
I. Title
941'.085'092

ISBN 0 7502 2294 8

Typeset in England by Malcolm Walker, Kudos Design.
Printed and bound in Italy by G. Canale & C.S.p.A.

Picture acknowledgements
The publishers would like to thank the following for allowing their pictures to be reproduced in this publication: Camera Press 5 (top), 7, 9, 20, 31, 35, 38 (both), 44, 45 (top); Getty Images/Fox Photos 15; Popperfoto 12 (bottom), 13 (bottom), 14, 39, 45 (bottom); Rex Features, London *cover*, 1, 6 (both), 10, 12, 13 (top), 16, 17, 18 (both), 19, 21, 22, 23 (both), 27 (both), 28, 29, 30, 33, 36, 37, 40, 41, 42, 43; Topham Picturepoint 4, 5 (bottom), 8, 11, 24, 25, 26, 32, 34 (both).

Contents

Titles and Tears

Diana Spencer was not born a princess. She did not even become 'Lady Diana' until she was thirteen years old, when her grandfather died and her father became Earl Spencer. But the Spencers were one of the oldest and richest families in Britain. Their family had lived on the same estates at Althorp in Northamptonshire for 500 years.

Diana grew to be proud of her Spencer background, but as a small child it meant little to her. Her childhood was spent at Park House in Norfolk. She loved the comfortable, rambling old house, surrounded by rolling fields and woods, where she played with her two older sisters, Sarah and Jane, and her younger brother, Charles.

Baby Di. Like many upper-class babies, Diana spent more time with a succession of nannies than with her parents.

Above: *As children, Diana and her younger brother, Charles, were particularly close.*

Right: *Diana's father kept albums of photographs of his children as they grew up. This one shows Diana aged seven.*

But when Diana was just seven years old, a terrible shadow was cast across her life. Her parents divorced and her mother moved away to London. Diana felt abandoned and helpless. She never forgot the sound of her mother's car driving away that night. She hoped that her own children would never suffer a similar distress.

Home and School

Below: *Diana's father, Earl Spencer, with his second wife, Raine. Diana worshipped her father, but was very upset when he decided to remarry in 1976.*

Diana's first school was in King's Lynn, a town near her home. Though the classes were small and the teachers very caring, Diana always found school life difficult. Unlike her brother Charles, she did not shine in her work. She became quiet and shy, though she was especially kind and helpful to younger children.

Below: *Althorp (pronounced 'all trup'), to which Diana's family moved when she was fourteen. She found it spooky, 'like an old man's club, full of clocks ticking.'*

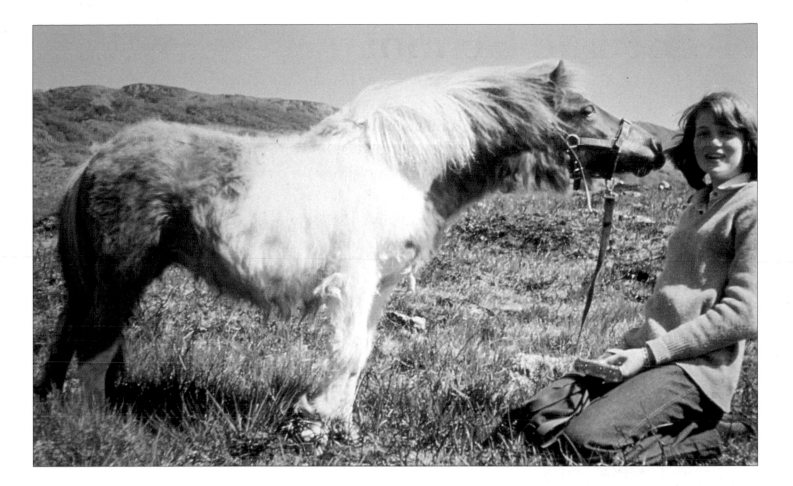

When she was nine years old, Diana's father sent her away to boarding school. She did not want to leave home and complained, 'If you love me, you won't leave me here!' However, she soon came to love the school, where she excelled at swimming, dancing and netball, and was awarded a prize for helpfulness. Best of all, she was allowed to have Peanuts, her pet guinea pig, with her at school.

During the school holidays at home at Park House, Diana sometimes met royalty. The Queen and her family became Diana's neighbours when they stayed nearby at Sandringham. The younger royal children, Prince Andrew and Prince Edward, would visit the Spencers at Park House to use their private swimming pool. In return, the Spencer children were invited back to play at Sandringham. The young Diana used to call the Queen 'Aunt Lillibet'.

Diana with her pony, Soufflé, in Scotland, in 1974. She loved animals, but an early fall from a horse put her off riding for life.

In Diana's own words: 'I loved being at school. I was very naughty in the sense of always wanting to muck about rather than sit tight looking at the four walls of the schoolroom.'

Children's Favourite

At thirteen years old, Diana started at West Heath, a senior girls' boarding school in Kent. She once said that she was 'thick as a plank'. This was not really true, though she left school with no exam passes.

After leaving school, Diana moved to London to share a flat with three friends. She took a cookery course, and did housework, waitressing and cleaning through a work agency called Solve your Problems. She also worked as a nanny, looking after young children for wealthy London families. The children loved her. Her talents were discovered, and before long she was working as a nursery school teacher.

The teenager with the cheeky smile. Diana was often in trouble at school and was once nearly expelled for going out at night on a 'dare'.

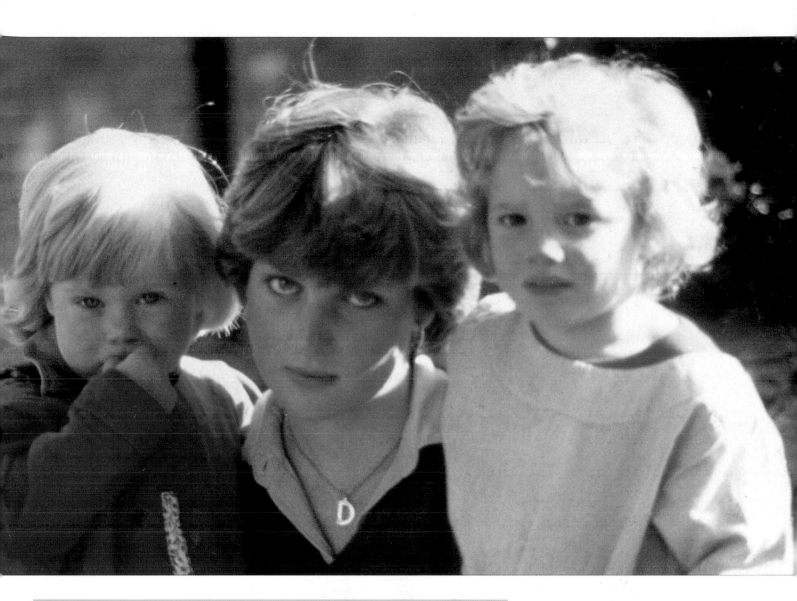

Voluntary Service

West Heath School's Community Service scheme had a lasting effect on Diana. Every week, she cleaned and made tea for an old lady in Sevenoaks. On Tuesday evenings, she and her friends visited a local mental hospital to help look after the patients. Diana's father had once told her to treat everyone as an equal.

'Miss Diana' with children at the Young England Kindergarten. Her musical and dancing talents were much in demand in the classroom.

Royal Romance

Diana's happy-go-lucky life in London did not last long. In July 1980, when Diana was just 19 years old, she and Prince Charles were guests together at a week-end party. As they chatted, the Prince, who was grieving the death of his great-uncle Lord Mountbatten, was touched by her sympathy and understanding. He invited her back to Buckingham Palace the next day. She refused – but other invitations followed, and before long a romance began to develop.

The Prince had once said that 30 was the ideal age to 'settle down'. Now he was nearly 33 years old and still unmarried. Newspaper stories often linked his name with other girlfriends. But when Diana began to appear at Charles's side, many people sensed that this time it was for real. They certainly hoped so. There was something fresh and natural about 'Lady Di', and her shy glance quickly captured everyone's hearts. To great excitement, the engagement was announced in February 1981.

Home to her flat in London. Once the secret was out, Diana's every movement was followed by the press.

Charles and Diana announce their engagement. 'With Charles at my side, I cannot go wrong,' she said.

In Diana's own words: 'He said, "Will you marry me?" I remember thinking, "This is a joke", and I said, "Yeah, OK", and laughed. He was deadly serious. He said, "You do realize that one day you will be Queen." A voice said to me inside, "You won't be Queen, but you'll have a tough role."'

A Fairy-tale Wedding

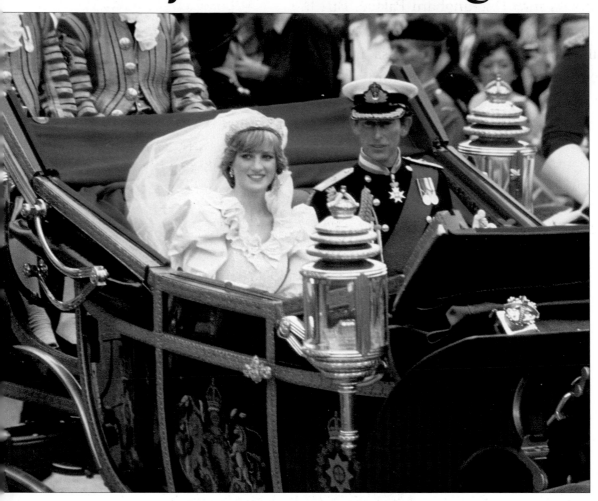

Returning to the Palace. The wedding was a very British celebration, full of pomp and pageantry.

Charles and Diana were married on 29 July 1981. Huge crowds gathered along the procession route between Buckingham Palace and St Paul's Cathedral, hoping for a glimpse of the royal couple. As the procession of carriages appeared, they cheered and waved flags. Meanwhile, 750 million people all over the world gathered in front of their television sets to watch the live broadcast of the ceremony.

The Archbishop of Canterbury, in his sermon, described the wedding as 'the stuff of which fairy-tales are made'. For the public, it all seemed to go without a hitch — except, that is, when Diana 'fluffed her lines' by repeating Prince Charles's first names in the wrong order.

In private, though, Diana was in distress. After the engagement, she had moved into Buckingham Palace. But life there seemed strange, cold and unfriendly. She began to be regularly sick with an illness called bulimia nervosa and lost a lot of weight. How she missed the fun and freedom of her old life in the flat with her friends! Surely, she hoped, things would improve once the wedding was over.

Just a small selection of the many souvenirs which people bought to help them remember this very special day.

On the balcony at Buckingham Palace. 'Give her a kiss,' people shouted, and the Prince, eventually, did.

Shy Di

With her marriage to Prince Charles, Diana ceased to be just 'Lady Di'. She was now 'Her Royal Highness the Princess of Wales'.

In a very short time, and at only 20 years old, she had to adapt to married life while learning to be royal herself. Despite her privileged upbringing, it was not easy. With her naturally shy personality, she was sometimes upset by the mass of journalists and photographers who followed her every move. For the rest of her life, Diana would have little privacy.

The royal couple in Australia on their first major overseas tour. Diana was constantly surprised by how many people would turn out to see her.

Grand formal occasions, such as palace dinners for important visitors, could be even more terrifying. She had so much to learn! On one occasion, she did not know who the gentleman sitting opposite her was. 'That,' said her husband, 'is the Chancellor of Germany, one of the most powerful men in the world.'

Diana felt more relaxed on visits like this, to the Great Ormond Street Hospital for Sick Children. She tried hard to ignore the constant click of cameras behind her.

A Princess in the Kitchen

Diana often felt uneasy in royal company. It is said that at Balmoral, the Queen's Scottish home, she used to hang around the kitchens chatting to the staff instead. A servant once pointed to the door and said, 'Through there, Ma'am, is your side of the house; through here is our side.'

Royal Roles

Despite her shyness, Princess Diana was keen to start work as a member of the royal family. She began to go on royal visits with Prince Charles. 'I wanted us to share everything together. I thought that we were a very good team,' she said. But wherever they went, it was Diana the people cheered, and poor Prince Charles was left collecting flowers to pass on to her.

The Prince and Princess at one of Charles's polo matches. 'We make a good team,' she said.

The royal family had done wonderful work for charity for a long time. Somehow, though, they still seemed remote from ordinary people's problems. Diana was different. She took a real personal interest in those she met. Polite handshakes were not enough for her; she longed to touch people, and was not afraid to hold hands and hug those in distress. This was Diana's special gift, and people loved her for it. As an Australian later said, 'She was the human face of royalty.'

Of all her duties, it was visits like this, to a school for disabled children, which meant most to Diana.

In Diana's own words: 'I remember when I used to sit on hospital beds and hold people's hands. People used to be sort of shocked because they said they'd never seen this before. To me it was quite a normal thing to do.'

Motherhood

Princess Diana's father once said, 'It will be a lucky baby who has Diana as a mother.' There was not long to wait. Prince William was born in June 1982, and Prince Harry was born two years later.

Of all the roles Diana took on, being a good mother was by far the most important to her. Remembering her own unhappy childhood, she promised never to let her children feel unwanted. When she and Prince Charles were due to leave for a tour of Australia, she refused to go without Prince William. This was unheard of for the royal family, but she got her way.

Below: *June 1989, and a barefoot Diana wins the mothers' race at Wetherby School, which Princes William and Harry attended.*

Above: *Diana proudly leaves hospital with the newborn Prince Harry, September 1984.*

Other royal mothers may have been affectionate with their children in private, but Diana loved to hug them in public. 'Cuddles have no nasty side-effects,' she said.

As far as possible, Diana wanted her children to live a normal life. She chose schools that were near home so that she could join in parents' activities with the other mums. Dressed in jeans and trainers, the children went with her on trips to theme parks and to see the latest movies at the cinema. Once William, the future king, was in his teens, Diana discussed everything with him. It was his idea for her to sell off many of her dresses to raise money for charity.

Diana was always game for a laugh with her sons. They all enjoyed the water ride at a children's theme park in 1993.

19

The Hidden Pain

To many people, Princess Diana's life must have seemed magical. She appeared to have everything anyone could wish for – beauty, wealth, popularity, two lovely children and a caring husband.

In Diana's own words: 'Bulimia is like a secret disease. You inflict it upon yourself because you don't think you're worthy or valuable. You fill your stomach up four or five times a day, and it gives you a feeling of comfort.'

Princess Diana had a remarkable ability to cover up her sorrow in public. But sometimes, however hard she tried, her true feelings showed through.

But secretly, Diana was suffering. After both her children were born, she had post-natal depression, an illness which leaves new mothers feeling very tired and low. No one else in the royal family had suffered from this problem, and they seemed unable to understand or help. Despite her busy and glamorous lifestyle, Diana often felt lonely.

It seemed to Diana that, however hard she tried, no one close to her ever said 'thank you' or 'well done'. She began to feel rejected, just as she had as a child. Diana also felt that she was growing apart from her husband. Her bulimia illness returned and she became very thin. People noticed, and the newspapers began to hint that something had gone seriously wrong in her life.

By 1992, the distance between Charles and Diana was plain for all to see. She always found formal events, like this, particularly difficult.

The Princess and the Press

However awful Diana felt privately, she knew that 'the show must go on'. She quickly learned to cover up her inner feelings with an amazing show of happiness. The press loved her. She was treated like a film star. Diana was the most photographed woman in the world.

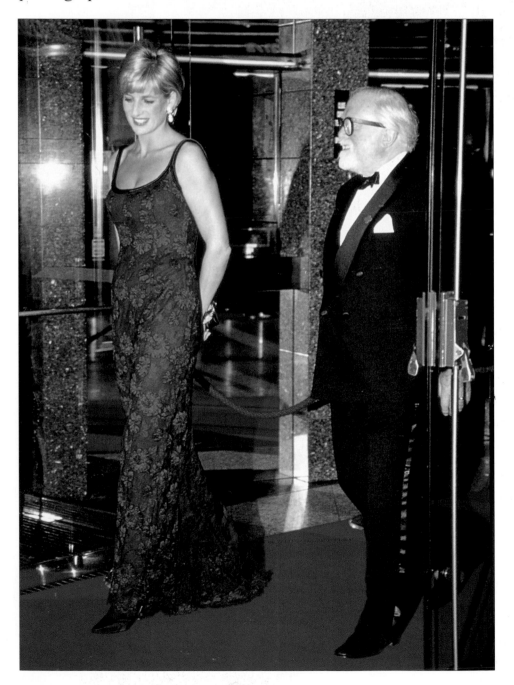

Diana arriving for a film premiere with Sir Richard Attenborough. Attenborough, a famous actor and director, coached Diana in public speaking to help her with her charity work.

Left: **With the opera singer Luciano Pavarotti. Many of the greatest names in show business and the arts became personal friends of the Princess**

Diana's tall, graceful figure stood out in a crowd whatever she wore. But she had a perfect sense of style, and knew how important it was to look just right for every occasion. Her specially designed dresses became famous, and much copied, the world over. Magazines competed to see who could get the best pictures of Diana, knowing that a good picture would sell thousands of extra copies.

At times, all this attention became too much for Diana. She tried to persuade photographers not to pursue her. When that did not work, she tried to shake them off, slipping out of back doors, hiding her face behind bags, and driving off at speed. But Diana knew that she could never entirely escape their attention. Nor did she always wish to – she depended on the press to publicize her charity work.

Right: **June 1997, at the Royal Albert Hall for a concert. With good reason, Diana was often called 'the world's most beautiful woman'.**

'The Glums'

By the early 1990s, Princess Diana was showing the strains of ten years in the spotlight. There were increasing rumours about a breakdown in her marriage to Prince Charles. The couple seemed to spend less and less time together. Prince Charles was said to have renewed his friendship with a former girlfriend, Camilla Parker-Bowles, while Diana's name was linked with various other men. When Charles and Diana made a visit to South Korea in 1992, they both looked so miserable that the newspapers called them 'the glums'.

The Prince and Princess stand to attention at the National Cemetery in Seoul, South Korea, in November 1992. This was their final tour together.

The Queen was worried, too. Most of the newspaper reports were based on guesswork, and were often untrue. However, it was obvious that relations between the Prince and Princess were bad, and this was harming the popularity of the rest of the royal family. For Diana, who remembered her pain at her own parents' divorce, it was a personal disaster. Yet she agreed, reluctantly, to accept a formal separation from Prince Charles in December 1992.

How the newspapers announced the separation of Charles and Diana, on 10 December 1992. Diana described it as the saddest day of her life.

Going Public

Separated from Prince Charles, perhaps Diana hoped for a more normal life. It was not to be. The public's interest in her was as great as ever, and the 'rat pack' of journalists still would not leave her alone. At times, she felt a prisoner in her own home, unable to do or say anything without being criticized.

Some of Prince Charles's friends blamed Diana for the separation and hinted publicly that she was mentally ill. In fact, she was feeling stronger than ever, having at last conquered her eating problems.

Diana determined to fight back. Working through friends, she had already helped a journalist called Andrew Morton to write a book, *Diana, Her True Story*, to tell her side of events. Overnight, the book became a best seller. Later, she gave a television interview in which she spoke about her life, her troubles, her ideas about royalty and her hopes for her children. The royal family were horrified by the programme, but she won the sympathy and affection of millions.

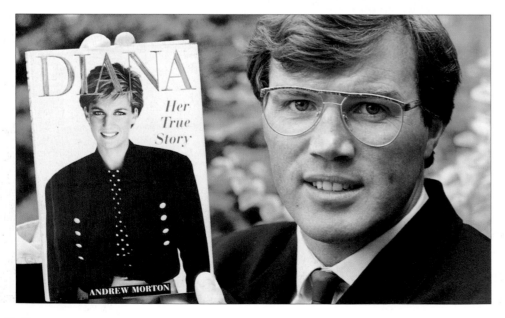

Author Andrew Morton with his book, based on information from Diana and her friends. Published in June 1992, the book hastened the separation of Charles and Diana.

Left: *On a visit to India with Prince Charles in 1990, Diana chose to pose alone in front of the Taj Mahal. It was through pictures like this, without Charles, that she first alerted the public to her unhappiness.*

Right: *In 1995, Diana was interviewed by Martin Bashir for the TV programme Panorama. The programme was kept secret until it was about to be shown.*

The Belle of the Ball

Princess Diana loved all types of music. Her tastes ranged from the solemn tones of Verdi's *Requiem* to the latest songs by her friend Elton John. She once complained of having to turn down the volume when her bodyguard was in the car, and earned the nickname 'Disco Di'. She had played the piano since childhood, and could entertain the crew of the Royal Yacht with a lively evening's music-making.

As a girl, Diana had hoped to be a ballet dancer, but grew too tall – 'I overshot the mark,' she said. Of the charities she helped, the English National Ballet was especially close to her heart. She became their Founder Patron in 1989, and over the next eight years she made hundreds of visits.

Dancing with John Travolta at the White House in 1985. 'For fifteen minutes, she made me feel like a prince. It was absolutely magical,' he said.

With dancers of the English National Ballet for a gala performance of Swan Lake, 1997.

Diana was involved in every aspect of the Ballet's work – from raising funds to choosing costumes and repertoire and looking after the welfare of the dancers. As with all her charity work, she did far more behind the scenes than was ever known to the public.

The Dancers' Inspiration

'**W**hen Diana came here, she always radiated a warmth, a grace, a happiness and a beauty – all things which are particularly special to dancers. She was completely at ease with the dancers and they were inspired by her.'
Jim Fletcher, English National Ballet.

Children's Champion

Princess Diana was so popular with the public that more and more organizations asked her for help. Over the years, she agreed to be patron or president of nearly a hundred charities. Patrons normally just attend occasional dinners and lend support to appeals. But Diana was different. She wanted to find out all about her charities, to meet the staff and the people they helped. Though she was always nervous of speaking in public, she took lessons from the actor Sir Richard Attenborough. She wrote her own speeches, and spoke movingly in support of many good causes.

The chance to sit on the Princess's knee brings a smile to the face of a young leukaemia patient.

Diana loved to visit children in hospital and often arrived unannounced. One girl said, 'I shall always remember her eyes – they were so beautiful, like the rest of her.'

Children's charities were especially close to Diana's heart. Barnardo's helps tens of thousands of young people and their families, especially those with special needs, and those suffering from poverty and abuse. When the Princess became President of the charity in 1984, she became actively involved. By 1996, she had attended 110 events, as well as making many private visits to see their work for herself.

My Smiling Friend

Eight-year-old Danielle Stephenson, who has a rare heart problem, first met Diana when the Princess popped in for a regular visit to the Royal Brompton Hospital. When Danielle was well enough, Diana invited her back to Kensington Palace for tea, and gave her a gold chain with a letter 'D' on it, like the one she had owned. For Danielle, Diana was 'the friend who always left us smiling.'

Being Herself

After Diana separated from Prince Charles, there were fewer royal duties for her to perform. This gave Diana the chance, which she had long wanted, to do more charity work.

To begin with, she tried to support all the charities of which she was patron. But with so many appeals for help, it was impossible to give them all the time and attention they deserved. In 1996, she reluctantly gave up being patron of all but six charities. At last she was able to concentrate on the issues that most concerned her.

At the Great Ormond Street Hospital, in 1997. She often followed up her visits to sick children with letters, cards and presents.

Always a regular hospital visitor, Diana was sometimes moved to tears by the sight of young children in pain. Both her own sons had been patients at the Great Ormond Street Hospital for Sick Children. Diana's involvement with the hospital helped them to raise huge sums of money for the Hospital (£54 million in only two years). She was also a regular visitor.

Diana's presence always had a wonderful effect on children. One mother recalled, 'During the time she spent with us, it was clear that to her nothing else in the world mattered. Her warmth helped us to smile again.'

Diana showed her deep compassion by wrapping her arms round people and hugging them.

On the Streets

Left: *In March 1997, Diana met Dave and Portia while visiting Centrepoint's cold weather project in King's Cross, London. The shelter provides food, beds and help for 47 homeless young people.*

As Princess Diana drove around London, she was often sad to see people begging on the streets, or sleeping out in all weathers in doorways and under bridges. During the 1980s and 1990s, many people had enjoyed opportunities and riches like never before. But here was another side of life, largely hidden from view, which Diana was determined to tell people about.

Right: *Diana speaking on behalf of the Centrepoint charity in 1995. Though she never felt at ease with public speaking, she knew how much good her words could do.*

Centrepoint

Centrepoint

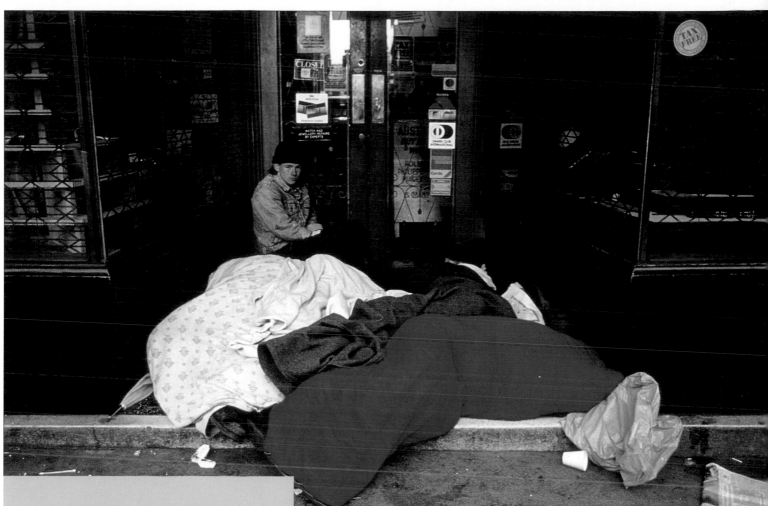

Sleeping rough. Diana was horrified to find some people as young as 11 years old sleeping on the streets.

Centrepoint

To the end of her life, Diana worked for Centrepoint, a charity that helps homeless young people. Diana liked the charity's positive approach: providing hostels and food, but also helping homeless people to find permanent homes and work.

As in all her work, the Princess became involved with helping people in private as well as in public. Often she would slip secretly out of Kensington Palace and visit night shelters for homeless people. Sometimes she took Prince William and Prince Harry along too, to chat or play cards with the people there. 'I want them to have an understanding of people's feelings, people's distress and people's hopes,' she said.

A Helping Hand

Some charities are more well known than others and are therefore easier to raise money for. But Princess Diana, typically, went out of her way to support the less-known causes that are usually ignored.

Cancer and Aids are diseases that many people do not even like to think about. They cause great pain, not only to sufferers but to families and friends who might have to watch their loved ones slowly die. As President of the Royal Marsden cancer hospital, Diana regularly comforted dying people. By auctioning seventy-nine of her dresses in June 1997, she raised almost £3 million to help patients.

Diana comforts an Aids patient at the Middlesex Hospital in July 1991. She was a good listener, and seemed instinctively to know how other people felt.

Diana had first become involved with Aids ten years earlier. At that time, many people refused to touch Aids sufferers in case they caught the disease. Diana not only touched them, she warmly held hands and hugged them. Her concern about Aids became very personal when she helped nurse a friend, Adrian Ward-Jackson, through the last months of his life. She took Prince William to see him, and flew home from holiday to be with Adrian when he died. As so often, people's attitudes towards the disease changed thanks to Diana's involvement.

In Diana's own words: 'I would like to be a Queen in people's hearts ... someone's got to go out there and love people, and show it.'

Diana's gentle touch brought joy to people of all ages. For eleven years she was patron of the charity Help the Aged.

International Action

Left: *Shaking hands with a leprosy victim. Pictures like this helped to educate people about the disease.*

In her last few years, Princess Diana began to take a lead in worldwide humanitarian issues. She had so often been moved by the desperate conditions of people she met on her foreign travels. Now she knew how she could help.

Bottom: *Serving bean stew to refugees in Zimbabwe in 1993.*

After visiting a hospital in Indonesia, she became Patron of the Leprosy Mission. This Christian charity treats and cares for people with leprosy in developing countries. Leprosy is a terrible disease, causing deformity and blindness. Many people fear the disease, and sufferers are often rejected even by their own families. But it can be cured if caught soon enough.

Diana helped to raise funds at home and visited leprosy hospitals in Mozambique, Nepal and India. Photographs of her, the most glamorous woman in the world, shaking hands with sufferers helped to dispel for ever the myths about leprosy. In December 1995, she was awarded the 'Humanitarian of the Year' award in New York 'for her work with the ill, the suffering and the downtrodden'.

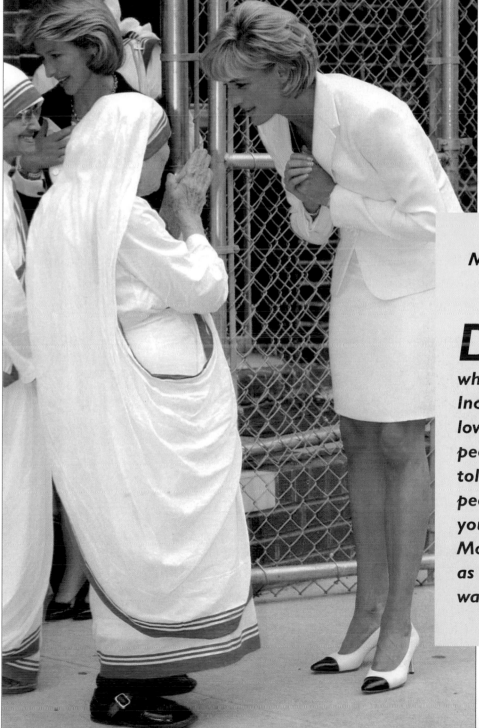

Diana had a lifelong admiration for Mother Teresa. This was the last time they met, in New York in June 1997.

Mother Teresa meets Diana

Diana and Mother Teresa were so different, yet when they met in Calcutta, India, they shared a common love of poor and outcast people. Mother Teresa once told Diana, 'To heal other people you have to suffer yourself.' When Diana died, Mother Teresa described her as 'a very great friend who was in love with the poor'.

Explosive Issues

With the divorce from Prince Charles finalized in 1996, Diana lost the title 'Her Royal Highness', and became officially 'Diana, Princess of Wales'. But in some ways, the last few months of Diana's life were amongst the busiest, and perhaps the happiest, of her life. She seemed to radiate a new energy, enthusiasm and joy.

Diana's wish to become a 'humanitarian ambassador' was being taken seriously by Britain's Prime Minister, Tony Blair. And she had a new cause to fight for – landmines. An estimated 100 million landmines are scattered across sixty countries, and nobody knows exactly where they are. Every fifteen minutes, innocent victims, mostly women and children, are killed or suffer terrible injuries from exploding mines.

Wearing protective clothing, Diana walks through a minefield in Angola. Some people criticized her for meddling in politics. 'I am not a political figure,' she said. 'I come with my heart.'

Diana was shocked by the terrible injuries she saw in Angola and Bosnia. Working a fifteen-hour day, she insisted on spending at least thirty minutes with every victim she met.

In Bosnia

'**O**ne boy took off his boots to show what his feet looked like. But he didn't have any feet left. Diana picked him up in her arms. There were no photographers there. She was not showing off. It was genuine impulse ... instinctive.' Lord Deedes.

In January 1997, Diana visited Angola as a Red Cross volunteer to find out more about the problem. The photographs of her walking across a minefield brought the horror home to the whole world. In August, she went to Bosnia. There she met victims and urged the world's governments to ban mines for ever. Sadly, it was to be her last mission.

A Tragic End

By August 1997, Princess Diana had at last put all her personal sorrows behind her. Following her trip to Bosnia, she was about to launch a new international campaign against landmines. Then it was off on holiday with her new friend Dodi Fayed. People talked of a possible romance. Would Diana remarry? Was this her chance to move abroad, as she had often wished, and live in the USA with Dodi? We shall never know.

On Sunday 31 August, people awoke to incredible news. Diana, Dodi and their driver had been killed in a terrible car crash in Paris. All over the world, stunned families stared in disbelief at their television screens as the details began to emerge.

To the end, Diana was hunted by the press. Here they caught up with her while she was on holiday with Dodi Fayed, a few days before their deaths.

Diana had spent a last evening with Dodi before preparing to fly back to be with her sons. As the couple left the hotel where they had dined together, they were pursued at high speed by a group of photographers on motorbikes. As the car entered a tunnel in the city centre, the driver lost control and the car crashed into a concrete pillar. The driver and Dodi were killed instantly, and Diana's bodyguard was seriously hurt. Diana herself was rushed to hospital with massive chest injuries. In the early hours of Sunday morning, she died.

The tangled wreckage of the car in which Diana and Dodi died. Though the driver had been drinking, we may never know exactly what caused the crash.

The World Mourns

For sixteen years, Diana appeared almost daily in the newspapers and on television. She had become, as no one else before, a part of everyone's lives. People who had never met her felt as if they had lost a close friend. Men, women and children openly broke down and cried. Never before had there been such public grief.

The royal family stayed at Balmoral, their Scottish home, helping the young princes to come to terms with their mother's death. Plans for the funeral were made and remade as the monarchy tried to stay in tune with public feeling. On television the Queen described Diana as 'an exceptional and gifted human being'. Diana's death, even more than her life, may have changed the role of royalty for ever.

Princess Diana's coffin enters Westminster Abbey followed by (left to right) Prince Charles, Prince Harry, Diana's brother Charles, Prince William, and the Queen's husband, the Duke of Edinburgh.

Above: *A sea of flowers placed in front of Kensington Palace, where Diana had lived. So many people wished to place tributes that thousands of flowers had to be specially flown into Britain.*

The following Saturday, millions lined the London streets or gathered together to watch the funeral on television. Diana's brother Charles described his sister as 'the unique, the complex, the extraordinary and irreplaceable Diana, whose beauty, both external and internal, will never be extinguished from our minds.' The crowds outside began to clap. Soon the congregation inside took up the applause. No one had ever clapped at a funeral before. But then no one before had ever seen the like of Diana.

Right: *Her final resting place. Princess Diana is buried on an island in the lake at Althorp House, the ancestral home of the Spencer family.*

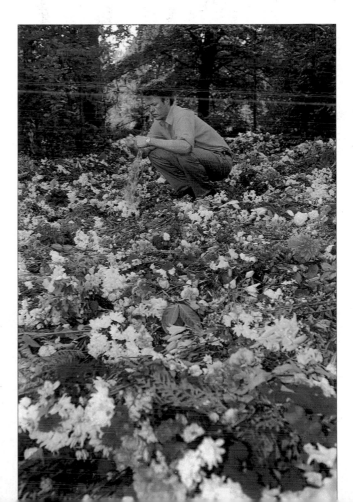

Glossary

Aids 'Acquired Immune Deficiency Syndrome', a disease that prevents the body resisting illnesses.

Ambassador Someone who represents a country abroad.

Auctioning Selling to whoever will pay the most.

Boarding school A school where the pupils live and study during term times.

Bulimia nervosa An illness in which people over-eat and then make themselves sick.

Community service A scheme for giving unpaid help to local people.

Deformity Out of shape as a result of injury or illness.

Developing countries Poor countries whose industries are still growing.

Dispel Get rid of.

Estates Lands and farms.

Extinguished Put out like a light, got rid of.

Formal separation An agreement, made by law, to live apart.

Glamorous Smart, rich and exciting.

Humanitarian Done for the good of human beings.

Instinctively Done without thinking, by instinct.

Leprosy A disease of the nerves and skin, which causes the skin to harden.

Leukaemia A disease of the blood which often causes early death.

Monarchy Royalty, the royal family.

Political To do with politics or the running of a country.

Pomp and pageantry Dignified, showy events, like processions.

Sermon A short talk during a church service.

Unannounced Without anybody knowing in advance.

Upper class From an important, titled or rich family..

Work agency A business which helps people find jobs doing the work they like.

Diana's Charities

Princess Diana worked for a great many charities.
These are a few of the organizations with which she was most closely associated.

Barnardo's
Registered Office, Tanners Lane, Barkingside, Ilford,
Essex IG6 1QG   Tel. 0181 550 8822

British Red Cross
9 Grosvenor Crescent, London SW1X 7EJ
Tel. 0171 235 5454 Internet address: redcross.org.uk

Centrepoint
Bewlay House, 2 Swallow Place,
London W1R 7AA   Tel. 0171 629 2229

English National Ballet
Markove House, 39 Jay Mews, London SW7 2ES
Tel. 0171 629 2229
Internet address: www.ballet.org.uk

**Great Ormond Street Hospital for
Sick Children**
London WC1N 3JH   Tel. 0171 405 9200

Help the Aged
St. James's Walk, Clerkenwell Green,
London EC1R 0BR   Tel. 0171 253 0253
Internet addres: http://www.helptheaged.org.uk

Leprosy Mission
Goldhay Way, Orton Goldhay, Peterborough PE2 5GZ
Tel. 01733 370505
Internet address: http:\\www.leprosymission.org/

National Aids Trust
188–196 Old Street, London EC1Z 9FR
Tel. 0171 814 6767
Internet address: www.nat.org.uk.\nat\

Royal Marsden Hospital NHS Trust
Fulham Road, London SW3 6JJ
Tel. 0171 352 8171

Important Dates

1961 Diana Spencer born at Park House,
Sandringham, Norfolk.

1968 Her parents divorce.

1974 Becomes 'Lady Diana' when her
grandfather dies.

1979 Works as nanny and nursery teacher in
London.

1981 Marries Prince Charles and becomes Princess
of Wales.

1982 Prince William born.

1984 Prince Harry born.

1989 Holds hands with leprosy victims in
Indonesia.

1990 Photographed looking sad and lonely
while in India.

1992 Andrew Morton publishes *Diana: Her True
Story.*
Diana agrees to a formal separation from
Prince Charles.

1995 Gives TV interview on *Panorama.*

1996 Divorced from Prince Charles.
Decides to concentrate on six charities.
Given the 'Humanitarian of the Year' Award
in New York.

1997 Visits Angola and Bosnia for the
landmines campaign.
Killed with Dodi Fayed in a car crash
in Paris.

Index

Numbers in **bold** refer to pictures as well as text.